CHURCH PEOPLE BEWARE!

Sermons For Pentecost (Middle Third)
Cycle A Gospel Texts

BY WILLIAM J. CARL III

C.S.S. Publishing Co., Inc.
Lima, Ohio

CHURCH PEOPLE BEWARE!

Copyright © 1992 by
The C.S.S. Publishing Company, Inc.
Lima, Ohio

All rights reserved. No part of this publication may be reproduced, stored in a retrieval system, or transmitted in any form or by any means, electronic, mechanical, photocopying, recording, or otherwise, without the prior permission of the publisher. Inquiries should be addressed to: The C.S.S. Publishing Company, Inc., 628 South Main Street, Lima, Ohio 45804.

Library of Congress Cataloging-in-Publication Data

Carl, William J.
   Church people beware! : sermons for Pentecost (middle third), cycle A Gospel texts / by William J. Carl III.
     p.   cm.
   ISBN 1-55673-426-3
   1. Pentecost season — Sermons. 2. Bible. N.T. Matthew — Sermons. 3. Presbyterian Church — Sermons. 4. Sermons, American. I. Title.
BV4300.5.C37   1992
252'.6—dc20   92-9067
                                                                            CIP

To my wife
Jane Alexander Carl
who has always
known how to speak
the truth in love

Table Of Contents

Preface   7

Proper 12   9
Pentecost 10
Ordinary Time 17
   The Problem With Finding The Kingdom
   Matthew 13:44-52

Proper 13   15
Pentecost 11
Ordinary Time 18
   You Provide The Bread
   Matthew 14:13-21

Proper 14   21
Pentecost 12
Ordinary Time 19
   The Problem With Miracles In Our Time
   Matthew 14:22-33

Proper 15   29
Pentecost 13
Ordinary Time 20
   The Faith Of Outsiders
   Matthew 15:21-28

Proper 16   37
Pentecost 14
Ordinary Time 21
   Rocky
   Matthew 16:13-20

Proper 17   43
Pentecost 15
Ordinary Time 22
    Living Sacrifices
    Matthew 16:21-28 (C)
    Matthew 16:21-26 (L)
    Matthew 16:21-27 (RC)

Proper 18   51
Pentecost 16
Ordinary Time 23
    Straight Talk, Due Process And Grace
    Matthew 18:15-20

Proper 19   57
Pentecost 17
Ordinary Time 24
    Who's Keeping Score?
    Matthew 18:21-35

Proper 20   63
Pentecost 18
Ordinary Time 25
    The Unfairness Of God
    Matthew 20:1-16

Proper 21   71
Pentecost 19
Ordinary Time 26
    Church People Beware!
    Matthew 21:28-32

Lectionary Preaching After Pentecost   77

C — Common
L — Lutheran
RC — Roman Catholic

Preface

Sermons have a hard time living once they leave the pulpit and the gathered earshot of the people of God in the context of worship, especially as they make their way into a book. If it is true, however, that preachers should speak as if they are having a conversation with one person rather than firing off a scattershot of eloquent oratory, then perhaps it is possible, on occasion, to publish sermons on the printed page for individuals to read in the quiet of their own homes or offices. It is this rhythm of speaking and listening and almost pausing for the reader at points that makes the preached word in the pulpit come alive for the hearer.

These sermons were, without exception, all preached at First Presbyterian Church of Dallas. Slight amendments have been made here and there to lift them beyond local and regional colloquialism. All of these texts are appointed for the middle third of Pentecost, Cycle A. They are tough texts which lead, in some cases, to tough messages. But, since Jesus rarely pulled any punches, neither should we. That's why the titles of a couple of them include "The Problem with . . ." this or that. The title of the collection comes from the last one which calls all of us into question: "Church People Beware!" Jesus surely loved those of us who seem most steeped in religion; but he also challenged us with the greatest cautions and warnings since through us the people of God learn who God is.

My hope is that you will not only be edified and comforted by these sermons but confronted again with the great demand of the gospel and its terrific call to be faithful not only in our common ministry but in our Christian lives.

My thanks to my wife, Jane, to whom this book is dedicated, and my sons, Jeremy and David, who keep their father honest biblically, theologically and practically. Thank you also to my secretary, Lori Smallwood, whose advice and assistance have been indispensable. Thanks also to Fred Steiner for his encouragement in the publication of this book.

Proper 12
Pentecost 10
Ordinary Time 17
Matthew 13:44-52

The Problem With Finding The Kingdom

I don't know about you, but when I finished reading these parables of the kingdom, I wasn't so sure whether I really wanted to find the kingdom, which may be an odd thing for a preacher to say, I admit.

But think about it — everybody always makes such a big deal about finding the kingdom. Even Jesus. "Seek ye first the kingdom of God and . . . all these things shall be added unto you." Even Peter Marshall's mother said it when Peter left Scotland for good. "Dinna forget your verse my laddie, seek ye first the kingdom of God and his righteousness and all these things shall be added unto you."

That's what Christians are supposed to do: go around seeking the kingdom of God. Right? But has anyone ever explored the problems that come with finding this kingdom? There are lots of them and they are hidden right here in this particular text.

First of all, finding the kingdom is something that happens when you're not even looking for it. That's the way it was for C. S. Lewis. One day he just stumbled onto the kingdom. In fact, instead of seeking the kingdom, he was doing his best to try to avoid it. Listen to his own description:

You must picture me alone in that room . . . night after night, feeling . . . the steady, unrelenting approach of him whom I so earnestly desired not to meet. (Finally, in 1929) I gave in, and admitted that God was God, and knelt and prayed; perhaps, that night, the most dejected and reluctant convert in all England. (Edited by Hugh T. Kerr and John M. Mulder, "Conversions," Grand Rapids, Michigan, William B. Eerdmans Publishing Company, pp. 201-202.)

Not all of us are all that happy to have been caught by God. But here we are in church anyway, still trying like Lewis to sort out how we got here in the first place: teenage conversion, a grandparent's fervent prayers or did we just stumble into religion the way Lewis did long ago, holding God off as long as we could and then finally giving in?

It's not that it's wrong to search for the kingdom. That's what the merchant in the second parable was doing and what he found was so spectacular that he sold everything he had to buy it. Searching for something of great value is not bad in itself.

In Virginia there are Civil War buffs who go out with the latest metal detector equipment and search the battlefields for memorabilia. One we went with used to get so excited. He'd get up on a hillside and say, "Here is where it took place. It was such and such a day that this particular battle occurred. The battle lasted only 30 minutes but the fighting was fierce. The Yankee troops came up this hill and the Confederates caught them on the left flank and I think if we look right around here we might find something." It was almost eerie the way he would talk about it like Patton at Palermo. But, sure enough, we'd find some mini-balls and you'd think we'd found a million dollars the way he acted. That's the way merchants in Jesus' day were about pearls of great price. They'd travel to the Persian Gulf or as far as India trying to find one little pearl.

In a way we're all searching for that something that will answer all our questions and solve all our problems, aren't we? And for each one of us it's different. Aren't we all seekers, wrote George Buttrick, in one way or another? We're all looking for something more. "Money is good, but not without friendship; friendship is good, but not outside a higher devotion; devotion to art and music is good, but not without a clear conscience; a clear conscience is good but impossible without forgiveness. So the thoughtful (person) is ever dissatisfied with moderate joys and shortened goals." *(Interpreter's Bible,* vol. 7, Nashville, Abingdon Press, 1951, p. 420). We are all searching for something — not just for something more, but for something greater in our lives.

According to Jesus, the greatest of all is the kingdom. And it's not wrong to search for it. But the man in the first parable just stumbled onto the kingdom when he wasn't even looking for it. He found it plowing one day, one poor farmer working another man's field. While he was out there he hit the treasure box with his plow and probably at first didn't even know what he had hit. In those days there were no banks or really safe places to keep the family jewels and treasures, so when soldiers came sweeping through, taking over lands, people would quickly hide their fortune in the ground in a place that only they would know about in the hopes that someday they would return and find it.

It was a buried treasure like this that the man in the parable no doubt found. He wasn't out searching for it. The last thing in his mind as he went out to work that day was discovering enough to retire on while plowing a field.

Jesus' point here is that the unique thing about the kingdom is not its hiddenness, but its everydayness. If our eyes are open, we can stumble into the kingdom every day. That's why Jesus kept saying, "The kingdom of heaven is at hand. The kingdom of heaven is at hand." That is to say, it's all around us. It's not so much the fact that the bush was burning that caught Moses' eye that day. It was that any old bush would do on any old day of sheepherding.

The trouble with this bush and the treasure in this field is that it changes your life forever. It makes you do things you don't really want to do; like be really joyful which is not that easy for all of us. Some of us are permanent grumps. And if you're not one yourself perhaps, God forbid, you have to live with one or listen to one who calls everyday and nags about everything under the sun. You know what I'm talking about: folks who always see the dark side of everything and spoil everybody's fun. Did you see the cartoon recently with the two bureaucrats at the Federal Drug Administration? One is saying to the other, "Say, if laughter is the best medicine, shouldn't we be regulating it?" There's always someone trying to put a damper on things.

But, of course, there are others who seem too joyful, too happy all the time. Life can't be that good, that wonderful! And if that's the kind of joy that comes when we find the kingdom, then we don't want any part of it. It seems too frivolous and empty.

But as you would imagine, that's not the joy Jesus had in mind at all. He's talking here about real joy, deep joy, the kind that is always close to tears; like when a loved one dies and since she was suffering so much, we're happy that her suffering is over and she is now in the hands of God and we say to everyone who comes to the funeral, "It's a blessing," and we really mean it. But all the time we're fighting back the tears. This is real joy, deep joy when we feel life to the fullest. Here is the kind of joy that C. S. Lewis had in mind when he talks about his own conversion which he titled *Surprised by Joy*. "The word 'joy' is used by him in a special way and is not the same as happiness, gladness or pleasure. In fact, for Lewis it includes a measure of agony and grief, but if once experienced it is eagerly sought for again and again (Kerr, Mulder, p. 199)."

The trouble is not all of us are sure that we are really ready for this kind of joy and that's part of the problem with finding the kingdom: It asks too much of us. It has too much of an edge to it. And the edge really comes out in the third parable where God separates those who understand about the kingdom and live it in their lives and those who don't. The image he uses is one that the disciples would have understood immediately. It would have taken them back to the smell of the sea and the burn of the rope in their hands and the weight of the net as it was dragged through the water. The image of the kingdom here is not of treasures in fields or pearls of great price, but a gospel net that catches all of us, fish of every kind, red and yellow, black and white, whether we like it or not in our town and in this country, and the good are gathered into the boat and the bad are tossed away. How's that for an image of the kingdom? Folks of all kinds hanging around with whom we have to learn to live whether we like it or not. And the image of hell doesn't wait until the afterlife perhaps because some of us live in the hells of our own making right now. According to this parable of the kingdom, Judgment Day is everyday. *Now* is the net being gathered in and *now* selfishness is its own condemnation and deceit its own curse.

Do you see now the problem with finding or being found by the kingdom? Whether you stumble across it like the poor man in the field or search for it until you find it like the rich merchant in the marketplace or are caught by it like the fish of the sea, if you're normal at all, you're not really sure you're ready for its joy or its judgment.

But that's not the main problem with finding the kingdom. The main problem with finding the kingdom is that in the end it costs too much. Notice in both early parables, both men gave up everything they had to purchase what was the kingdom to them. Talk about a major gamble, the kind some savings and loans took around the country in the 1980s. But in this case, the two men in the parables gambled much more. Getting in on kingdom action costs you everything you have, says Jesus. That's how precious it is.

That's why you better think twice before you buy into it. Why? Because buying into the kingdom means giving up everything, especially old habits and ways of doing things that are destructive to ourselves and others. It means giving up the kind of stinginess that finds us holding back from God. That's what got Cain in trouble way back in the beginning of Genesis. He held back; he only gave God the dregs instead of the first fruits.

Do you see now the problem with the kingdom? It costs too much. How much does the kingdom cost? It costs you your whole life. And for some people, that's just a little too expensive.

Of course, it wasn't for the man in the field or the merchant in the marketplace. It wasn't for Albert Schweitzer or Mother Theresa or Peter or Paul. They gave up everything. Sold everything to have this one treasure in their hands. Was it because they saw in the kingdom the insearchable riches of Jesus Christ and realized that nothing they owned or had was worth losing out on that? Not even their lives? And suddenly finding the kingdom was no problem at all. Not a sacrifice at all. But sheer joy! Listen to Paul in Philippians: "But whatever gain I had . . . I count everything as loss because of the surpassing worth of knowing Christ Jesus my lord. For his sake I have suffered the loss of all things, and count them as refuse, in order that I may gain Christ and be found in him . . . (Philippians 3:7-9a).''

Here are the words of one who has found a great treasure, the greatest treasure of all. A treasure more precious than the Crown Jewels or the Taj Mahal. Here are the words of one who knows that in finding this kingdom, she has found a glimpse of God's will for her life. That's why we pray, "Thy kingdom come, thy will be done." And in finding God's will for our lives we have found our true destiny which is worth more than anything. Finding out why you and I are here on this earth is worth all the gold in the world.

How ever you may find the kingdom in your life, whether you stumble across it coincidentally in an everyday task — discover it finally after a life-long search or are caught up in it before you know what God has done to you — how ever you find the kingdom, I hope you don't pass up the chance to buy into it. All it will cost is your life. But it will be the greatest investment and the greatest adventure you've ever made.

The problem with finding the kingdom? With Jesus Christ it's no problem at all.

Proper 13
Pentecost 11
Ordinary Time 18
Matthew 14:13-21

You Provide The Bread

When I was growing up, church picnics were a big thing. I can still see it . . . long tables with white cloths strung out end to end. Plastic forks and knives, napkins and paper plates on this end. Pitchers of lemonade and iced tea on that end. In between assortments of meat dishes and vegetables down here; various salads and desserts down there. Plenty of rolls and butter. Makes me hungry just thinking about it. In some rural churches they were an all-day affair. People came to church early and left late. They ate and played and sang together — true Christian fellowship. There always seemed to be plenty of food left over.

Looks like our story of the feeding of the 5,000 is no different. Just another church picnic only a little bigger. No one announced ahead of time that on a certain hill at 4:00 in the afternoon "we will gather together with Jesus to eat." No one announced what to bring. A-H bring vegetables. No one even organized it the way our church finally did. We had to. For a while everyone would bring the same thing. Everyone would bring dessert, and the children would be sick for two days. Or they would all bring salads and the dieticians would smile — all that good roughage, great for regularity. No. At the feeding of the multitude, no one was expected. The whole thing was impromptu. It just happened.

There they were listening to Jesus' sermon, enthralled with Jesus' words, and some stomachs started grumbling. So Jesus, deciding that he had talked long enough, began to be concerned about the people's hunger. He stopped and said, "Let's feed them." You see, our religion is not merely a spiritual, but a physical matter as well. Our faith is not in a God who remains mysterious in some heaven we can't see. Our faith is in a God who became a man, who got hungry and thirsty even as we do today. In Buttrick's words, "Not a marionette dropped heaven or angel come slumming." He was very man of very man who knew our hurts. When he cut his finger it bled. He asked for water from the woman at the well and on the cross he said "'I thirst.'" So Jesus took compassion. He always has since it's his nature. It's the nature of God. "They don't need to go away. You give them something to eat."

In the wilderness God provided manna for the Israelites who escaped from Egypt. God told pouting Elijah to get up and eat. In an upper room, he sat at a table, not too different from the one in every church, and says to each of us, his poor, dear children, broken and hungry, "take, eat." All of the stories reveal a very simple fact — that God Almighty is concerned about lunch. And because of that, Christ believed in feeding the hungry. He knew what real missionaries have always known — that an empty stomach rarely leads to a soul redeemed for Christ, even before Maslow created his hierachy of needs. Christ takes compassion on us in our human predicament.

But the compassionate thing to do is not always the practical thing to do. The practical thing to do in this case is to send the people away. So the disciples did the only thing left for them to do: they met and reported to Jesus. "We have looked at the budget, taken a tally and concluded that there's not enough here to feed all these people. Even if we send out, the closest fried chicken place is 10 miles away. Not even Dominos can handle a crowd like this. Let's send them home." Good practical advice.

Well, Jesus didn't even put it to a vote. He seems to have made up his mind ahead of time. "Come now. You can do better than that. Work with what you've got." No matter how poor you think your resources are. No matter how deep the trouble, work with what you've got. "How many loaves have you? Work with what you've got." You are in some deep trouble. There seems to be no way out. You are at the lowest point and Christ turns to you and asks, "How many loaves have you? Examine your resources."

He says to the disciples, "Work with what you've got." By the way, what have you got anyway? They replied, "five loaves and two fishes." It's not much by any standard. Not for 5,000 people. People of lesser faith in the power of God would have said, "Well, I see your point." But Jesus isn't put off by anyone, least of all you and me scurrying about worrying whether or not we will raise the budget this year. Christ is not interested in budgets. He is interested in people growing in the faith and trusting in his power. Budgets are only a barometer of how people are growing in the faith and trusting in his power. I sometimes wonder if those who started the Stewpot here at First Church read this passage every morning. The hungry faces were about the door peering in as they are in every town in every age. Some with good reason said, "We'll never be able to do it on $300." Others heard the voice of God echoing through the ages. "You provide the bread. Let me take care of the miracle." And by God's grace, $300 has grown to nearly $500,000 and a few loaves have grown into hundreds of thousands of loaves as folks all over the city continue to provide the bread which God blesses and spreads to the poor and hungry of downtown Dallas. You send your money in and God does something with it.

As a practical, reasonable Presbyterian, I have trouble with this idea. Even though I know it is right. As a practical, reasonable Presbyterian, I have trouble with Jesus. Jesus seems to believe too much in the power of God. I would rather hold back. Be realistic. I am much more like the 42-year-old president of the successful computer software company whose sign on his desk reads, "Never promise them pie in the sky until you see the bakery truck coming down the street." But that sign is too safe for Jesus. He would knock it off the desk just as surely as he challenged his disciples that day. He is much more than entrepreneur, the risk taker. He is always out ahead of us, calling us forward challenging us to be more than we think we can by the grace of God.

Or perhaps, he gives us such outlandish promises because he can in fact see the bakery truck way out in the distance. Because he knows the power of almighty God when it is unleashed in the midst of a giving people, a congregation that means to take the lead, a congregation that means to show its community, yea, even this country, what it is to sacrifice in the name of Christ. "How many have you?" says the Lord. "Not many" is our reply. "More than you think," says Jesus. "You don't have to send them away. Give them something to eat. You provide the bread, let me take care of the miracle. How many loaves have you? Work with what you've got." Do you see the risk involved when you follow this Christ? We all want to be one-talent people holding on for dear life to the few chips we have, while all the time Jesus wants us to make like the five-talent man. He wants us to bet the whole ranch on Beautiful Dreamer to show in the third. "You provide the bread. Let me take care of the miracle."

Perhaps William Barclay is right, an explanation that even a good post-Kantian, post-Newtonian, scientific secularist could buy. Perhaps he is right when he says that the focus of this story should not be on the loaves and the fishes, but on the hearts and souls of the people gathered. Perhaps the focus should not be on the miracle of the physical multiplication of loaves, but the miracle of selfish people becoming generous people. Maybe what happened was that the 5,000 did have some food and in the presence of Christ they opened up and began to share.

There was once a missionary in the Philippines who worked in the gold-mining communities of Bagio. He led many worship services in little huts that had been put up on stilts because of the monsoon rains. One Sunday he went up into a little hut only to find it packed with people. It was communion Sunday. In the front was a little table covered to the floor with white cloth. On it were a little piece of bread and a tiny Dixie cup filled with grape juice. He wondered whether these elements would be enough for this large group huddled together. But he forged ahead. He said the words over the bread and passed it around. Somehow, miraculously, a small corner of it came back. Then he took the little cup in his hand as he had held that silver chalice many times back in the states and said, "This cup is the new covenant in my blood. Drink ye all of it." He passed it around. It made it through the first two rows and came back. It was set on the table in front of him, empty. They looked at him smiling as if to say, "Produce some more now." He looked about frantically for a bottle of grape juice. There was none in sight. He prayed, "Lord, help me" and suddenly a little brown arm came up from under the table and snatched the cup off. The missionary smiled at the people nervously and then pulled up the cloth only to see a little Filipino man with a pitcher of water and four packages of grape fizzies! Dropping the cloth quickly, the missionary looked back at the crowd smiling confidently. Pretty soon a little brown arm came up and placed a full cup of grape juice on top of the table. And off they went with the rest of the service. "You provide the bread; let me take care of the miracle."

 What little thing can you do — a word of hope? A helping hand? Though it may seem useless to you against the vast needs of the world, do it. Whatever the deed, God will bless it and spread it. You and I are called to bring our tiny field to God's great sky, "our filament of wire to God's electric power. Thus the scientist brings his labored search, and God gives the flash that leads to new discovery. Thus the (composer) brings his pen and seeming poverty of thought and — suddenly the inspiration. Thus the saint brings" (her) own humble life and the world is somehow changed (George Buttrick, *Interpreter's Bible,* vol. 7, Nashville, Abingdon Press, 1951, p. 432).

What preacher who has spent a lifetime preaching in a pulpit has not known the frustration of a sermon that seemed limp on Saturday night, but soared Sunday morning by the power of the Spirit? "You provide the bread. Let me take care of the miracle," says the Lord.

And so it happened with a little man in North Carolina named Mr. Beam. He was a minister for a while in small country churches. Oh, how he loved to preach the Word, to stand before a little huddle of God's people and preach the Word from the Book. He considered it the greatest honor and privilege a person could ever have. But then he developed a problem with his throat. And that was the end of his preaching. It nearly broke his heart — the man who loved preaching so much.

When he died, he left all he had to a church in Charlotte for "purposes of evangelism" he said. What he left grew and grew and now, single-handedly supports the weekly television ministry. And it is said around Charlotte that in a single service on any given Sunday, more people hear the message of Christ than Mr. Beam ever preached to in a whole lifetime. "You provide the bread. Let God take care of the miracle."

Worry not about what little you have to give. Whatever it is, God will bless it and spread it to the glory of God's kingdom.

Don't worry about the future anymore. You provide the bread. Let God take care of the miracle.

**Proper 14
Pentecost 12
Ordinary Time 19
Matthew 14:22-33**

The Problem With Miracles In Our Time

If the truth be known, most of us would have to admit that we walk a very fine line between believing and not believing. There are times in our lives when, yes, we do seem to believe all these things we say about God when we read the Bible and sing the hymns in our own churches. There are even times when we'd say, yes, we feel close to God, whatever that means.

But there are also those desert times in our lives when we wonder whether or not we believe any of it at all anymore: God, Jesus, the church, discipleship — all of it seems like so much pie in the sky, a lot of sound and fury signifying nothing. It's especially true of miracles, isn't it?

The problem with miracles is that they don't seem to happen any more, so we're not sure we believe in them anymore. So we joke about the miracles in the Bible, especially these. We tell the one about the three preachers out fishing in the boat, two of which walk to shore on the water and when the third tries, sure enough, he sinks, and one of the two says to the other "You think we should tell him where the rocks are?" You can make the one who sank any denomination you want to, depending on your audience. But whatever way it's told, it's not a very ecumenical joke.

Or there's the one about the boy who came home from church and his mother asked him what he learned in Sunday school and he told her about Moses leading Israeli troops using the latest surface-to-air missiles against the Egyptians. And she says, "Are you telling the truth?" And he says, "No, but if I told you what the teacher said happened, you'd never believe me."

We don't know what to do with the miracles in the Bible, so we tell these same old jokes over and over. Or we try to explain them, doing our best to fit them into our view and experience of the world. So the waters didn't really part, in true Cecil B. DeMille fashion, say some scholars, but the wind blew on the shallow Reed Sea as it often does and the waters moved over a little at that moment. And Jesus didn't really multiply the loaves and fishes but opened the people's hearts to share the food they had brought and hidden in their coats or Peter had done a head count during the sermon and sent out for 5,000 box lunches to go.

Barclay says about this walking on the water story that Jesus was really at the edge of the shore since the *epi ten thalassan* could mean either "on the water" or "toward the water." It could mean that the wind had driven the boat to the northern shore of the lake, and Jesus, seeing his disciples "struggling in the moonlight . . . came walking through the surf of the shore" and so startled the disciples that they were terrified and thought he was walking on the water (William Barclay, *The Gospel of Matthew*, vol. 2, Philadelphia, Westminster Press, 1957, p. 117).

Or there is the even more fanciful attempt by the 18th century German theologian of the Enlightenment Period, Carl Friedrich Bahrdt, who suggested it's possible that there was some timber near the shore and that Jesus stepped on it and felt that it bore his weight and he approached the boat on it, clambering in beside the disciples, and the disciples who never saw things very clearly anyway, always saw more than was happening, passed on for posterity the story of Jesus' journey on the cedar wood as if the waves themselves had borne him up

(Ernst and Marie-Luise Keller, *Miracles in Dispute: A Continuing Debate,* trans. by Margaret Kohl, Philadelphia, Fortress Press, 1969, pp. 67-79). I call this one the "lumberjack log-rolling theory" which should change the joke from showing the dumb preacher where the rocks are to showing him where the logs are.

We can't believe in the miracles, so we either joke about them or we try to explain them rationally and in so doing, try to fit them into the world as we know it, but the explanations are often more ludicrous than the miracles themselves.

Of course, biblical literalists want us to believe that God had a magical touch in biblical days and some believe with healings that it still happens today. After all, the Israelites had it right with their view of the human being as a "psychosomatic unity, an indivisible amalgam of body and soul" whereby if either goes wrong, the other is affected. So the verb the New Testament uses for "save" means both to save and to heal and the word used for "Savior" can mean either Savior or physician.

Buechner, hardly an ultra-conservative, is right on this matter: "Ever since the time of Jesus, healing has been a part of the Christian tradition. In this century it has usually been associated with religious quackery or the lunatic fringe, but as the psychosomatic dimension of disease has come to be taken more . . . seriously . . . it has regained some of its former respectability (Frederick Buechner, *Wishful Thinking,* New York, Harper and Row, Publishers, 1973, p. 36)."

Another way of saying it would be you don't have to be a follower of Oral Roberts to believe in the miraculous healing power of God. You can even be a Presbyterian or a Methodist or a Baptist or an Episcopalian or a UCC or a Disciples or a Lutheran or a Catholic, even in today's world.

Certainly all things are possible with God and we want to believe when we are sinking, and sooner or later most of us feel like we are, whether or not we want to admit it. We all have that sinking feeling at one time or another in our lives even more than Garrison Keillor's 25 portly Lutheran ministers stuck out on the lake on Carl Krebsbach's pontoon boat which

Pastor Ingqvist suddenly realized was tipping bow to stern and slowly sinking into the lake as they discussed theology and shared their concerns about rural ministry. All the time Pastor Ingqvist kept noticing the boat tipping bow to stern deeper and deeper until one tip too many pitched several of the ministers right into the lake, a renewal of their baptism. "Eight of them took their step for total immersion (Garrison Keillor, *Leaving Home*, New York, Viking, 1987, pp. 103-108)."

Now that's a comical scene, especially the way Garrison Keillor tells it. But the sinking that Matthew is describing here isn't comical at all. It's the kind of sinking feeling you experience when you're waiting for the doctor's report on yourself or your loved one and sure enough, the doctor says what you were afraid he was going to say. It's the kind of sinking feeling you get when all your friends are dying around you and you feel all alone. Or, you're about to start in a new school and you're afraid you won't know anyone, or your marriage or your business or life itself, is on the rocks, and like Peter you want to cry out, "Lord, save me, I'm about to go under."

Yes, when we are sinking, we want to believe. It's more than "no atheists in foxholes" because we really genuinely want to believe, not just in God, that's easy enough, but that God really intervenes in our lives and our world. We want to believe in miracles, but we're not sure they really happen anymore. We want to believe, but we're not sure we can.

Then suddenly it hits us. The real problem with miracles is not that they don't happen. The real problem is they do. We just don't see them because they happen in ways that we don't think. Augustine had it figured out. Miracles, he believed, are occurrences which are contrary not to nature itself, but to what is known of nature. So, says Sockman, "I do not believe Christ did what he did by suspending or violating the laws which medical science has discovered to be valid. What he did do was to bring into use laws higher than modern science has yet charted (Ralph Sockman, *20 Centuries of Great Preaching*, vol. 10, edited by Clyde E. Fant Jr. and William M. Pinson Jr., Waco, Texas, Word Books, 1971, p. 176)."

But more than that, they are acts of God in this sense: "... history is the arena where God intervenes specifically from time to time," comforting us, pressing demands on us and judging us for our disobedience. "It is these extraordinary interventions which, properly speaking, are the miracles of the Bible . . . they are sufficiently startling, unusual and unexpected to call attention to themselves" and point as signs to the kingdom of God.

So Jesus' miracles of healing and feeding were not told as proof of God's kingdom, but as signs of it and as such only faith recognizes them as acts of God, for miracles don't prompt faith — faith helps us see miracles. Miracles, then, in the real sense, are "completely inaccessible" to human reason because their causes lie "solely within the will of God," and only faith can recognize this (Keller, *op. cit.* p. 21). Even the skeptical, doubting Reverend Lewis Merrill in John Irving's, *A Prayer for Owen Meany,* understood when he said that miracles don't cause belief; they don't make faith out of thin air; "you have to *already have faith* in order to believe in *real* miracles (New York, Ballantine Books, 1989, p. 524)."

The problem so many have with miracles today is that they think they prove something. But what do miracles really prove? Nothing. A thousand miracles would neither prove nor disprove Jesus' teaching. Miracles can neither make true teaching false nor false teaching true. Jesus understood this. That's why he kept downplaying the miracles. That's why he kept telling his disciples to keep quiet about them. You know . . . the Messianic Secret and all.

There are too many even in our day who think a miracle will show these unbelievers that God exists, but that's not the way miracles work. In Bruce Marshall's novel *Father Malachy's Miracle*, Father Malachy prays fervently that God would physically move an obnoxious dance hall on Edinburgh Street to the Bass Rock in the Firth of Forth. And sure enough, it happens. But instead of bringing reknown to himself and his church, the miracle is a source of embarrassment. Far from strengthening faith in God, it becomes the focal point of public ridicule. Even the police are angry over the disturbance of the peace it causes. "A pretty kettle of fish," says the bishop. "Umph! A miracle in the 20th century."

Bruce Marshall's theology is right on target in this novel. God is not some divine magician ready to pull rabbits out of every hat we offer up in prayer; and miracles do not produce faith. Only in faith do we even recognize them at all. Only in faith did Mary recognize Jesus at the empty tomb. Only in faith did the disciples recognize the stranger on the road to Emmaus. And how do real miracles come to us? Only when all seems lost and the limits of our human resources have been reached and passed, when all hope seems gone and there's nothing left but our faith in God.

It may happen in the dramatic turnaround of an incurable illness. It may happen in the sudden ability to face death unafraid when the illness still prevails and seems to hold you in its clutches to the very end and the miracle is that in the face of your own death you are never defeated. It may come in changed attitudes toward people and events. It may happen through us as the hungry are fed and the naked are clothed in our own churches. The movie *Always* argues that it happens through the thoughts placed in our minds by angels or loved ones now departed. Who knows how it comes? Whatever way it comes, I know it does as God intervenes at those points when we seem to be sinking the most. I think that that's what the biblical writers believed.

We know that miracles happen in occurrences that are unexplainable except to the eyes of faith. So the 19-year-old Khum Paot recounts her narrow escape from the Khmer Rouge in Cambodia after an arduous journey with 100 other refugees through miles of jungle, canals, mountains and rivers. Between them and freedom were Communist troops and "a stretch of jungle ground covered with thorns." At midnight the little party crossed a valley between two high mountain ranges. "We could see absolutely nothing," she told a missionary later. "We couldn't even see where to step." Then suddenly scores of fireflies swarmed into view, and by the glow of firefly light, they made their way to the next mountain.

At Kham Put refugee camp Khum Paot was invited to a Christian meeting. When she came in, she pointed to a picture on the wall of the chapel. "I know that old man," she said. "He's the one who led us to freedom." She'd never seen it before, but it was a picture of Jesus.

I don't know how these things happen. I just know they do and only the eyes of faith can see them. I don't know if the waters parted for Moses the way they did for Charlton Heston or what exactly happened by that boat with the disciples that day, but I can tell you this — you'll never convince them that God wasn't there. Whatever happened, God intervened and saved them. And it still happens today, in our world, in our time.

I know it's not easy to believe in miracles in our time. The problem with them is not that they don't happen. The problem is that they do. The question is do we have faith enough to see them and experience in them God's power and God's presence in our lives? Only you can answer that question for yourself.

Proper 15
Pentecost 13
Ordinary Time 20
Matthew 15:21-28

The Faith Of Outsiders

Have you ever had an inner emotional pain that would not go away? A depression that would come and go in waves? Sometimes it seemed like everything was completely normal and then it would come upon you totally unexpected. Perhaps it was related to something that happened in your childhood, something so awful that you couldn't tell anyone, not even your spouse or your best friend because in reality you weren't really sure you believed it yourself. Sometimes it would sneak into your dreams, dreams so bad that you wanted to wake but could not. But then during the day it was even worse, the wounded child inside you crying out, wanting to be healed.

Maybe it has something to do with awful past sins that you committed long ago but because you weren't Catholic and had no confessional to go to, you'd never told anyone about it, least of all a priest or a minister, never even discussed it with God although you were sure that God knew, since God knows everything. All this time you've been meaning to tell someone and ask for forgiveness and finally get it off your back.

Or maybe it's because you are the world's greatest worrier, with extra lines etched in your face to prove it. Every congregation has its champion worriers, worriers who can keep large ships afloat with their worrying. I know some who have gotten their children through college on one long four-year worry. Of course, sooner or later they realize that it wasn't the worrying that got their kids through since worrying is like rocking in a rocking chair; it gives you something to do but it doesn't get you anywhere. For some it's worse than that. For some, worry causes deep emotional pain.

Have you ever had that kind of deep anguish that will not let you go? So deep and painful that you wanted to scream? The Bible calls it demons. Today we call it by other more proper psychological names. Whatever it was, the Canaanite woman's daughter had it and she had it bad. It had gotten hold of her and would not let go. And her mother was rightly concerned, as any mother would be. Imagine if you were her mother, what would you have done?

There is something peculiarly scary when your child gets sick, so sick that it has to be taken to the hospital. Walk your way through any children's hospital and look at the concern on the parents' faces as their infant children or toddlers are hooked up to half the machines in the place or are being prepped for surgery. It touches your heart just to be in the same room with them. That's why the girl's mother was ready to try anything, even religion, which is the way most of us work. When all else fails, we turn to God. In this case, the woman had heard that a holy man was in town. One who had great powers to overcome all kinds of problems. Since nothing else had worked, she figured she'd better risk even talking to this Jew, even though she basically despised Jews. Canaanites and Jews had had it in for each other for a very long time. But the stories about this one were so remarkable, she figured it was at least worth a try.

When she saw him for the first time, he was with his disciples. Is he really the Son of God? she wondered. That's what they say. How simple and plain he seemed. Just like us. Have you ever noticed how celebrities always seem taller until you see them in real life? But he did look sturdy and strong, the signature of a life of carpentry. And what a preacher this one was! He could turn a phrase like no one you'd ever heard.

But not heavy with too much flowery or eloquent speech. No, he was simple, down-to-earth. His words cut straight and fast. His words have power, they say. He speaks with authority, they say. Not even been to seminary, they say. Sure knows scripture. Sure knows God. Sure knows people.

She stood there looking at him for a long time. There was something about him, the woman had to admit. There was only one problem, and thinking about it snapped her out of her trance. He was a Jew and Canaanites hated Jews more than Palestinians hate Israelis today and vice versa. Besides, what was he doing this far north? Just as there are certain neighborhoods in every American city, you just don't go into day or night, so there were regions where Jews didn't travel and Tyre and Sidon was certainly one of them.

Why was Jesus there? Perhaps he was looking for some respite from the crowds that had been growing steadily with each passing day. Perhaps he wanted some relief from the sanctimonious Pharisees who thought the whole world outside Judea was unclean and Jesus just needed some fresh air and some time to think and re-think where his mission was going.

I don't think the woman really cared why he was there. She needed help, so as he walked by she decided to yell, which was a gutsy thing to do. Women didn't talk to men openly like that, especially across racial barriers. And part of the problem is what she said. She yelled, "Have pity on me, Sir, Son of David!" which was not an appropriate thing for a Canaanite woman to say since "Son of David" was a title that gave expression to the national hopes of Israel. Her use of this term could have easily been misunderstood as sarcasm or a racial slur like "Hey Jew!" Little wonder Jesus ignored her. Wouldn't you if someone had yelled "Hey Honkey!" or "Hey Polack!" at you while you were walking down the street?

But she had heard that this man was different somehow. She had heard that he was the Son of God or something like that. At least that's what some of his followers said. But when she cried out, "Hey Jew!" that day Matthew says, "He answered not a word." Of course, it's possible that he didn't hear her at all; you know the way our loved ones and friends say that they can't hear us sometimes when we know that they hear a lot more than we think. Truth be known, we all hear what we want to hear, and sometimes it seems like God doesn't hear us at all, which is not true. God does hear. But God doesn't always reply. In fact, sometimes God seems so silent that it seems like he's not there at all. But that's not the case. Jesus was silent many times in his life. He was silent before Herod. He was silent before Pilate. Fact is, Jesus was probably silent more often than not. As a person who chose his words very carefully, my guess is that Jesus unnerved people the way he looked at them with those penetrating eyes, searching their hearts and his own with all his silence.

The silence of God unnerves us all. When we want help and want it now, why does God seem so silent? There are times in all our lives when we experience the *deus absconditus,* the absence of God. And finally, some of us just give up — give up on God, each other and life itself.

But not the Canaanite woman who teaches us and Jesus about the faith of outsiders. In a way, she is becoming a pest like the young woman in the John Wayne movie where John Wayne plays the part of Rooster Cogburn, the broken down drunken marshall the woman hires to stalk and kill her father's murderer. At first, Cogburn tries to ignore her, then send her away, but there is no way to get rid of her. That's the way the Canaanite woman was. Even the disciples try to send her away.

She is very much like the woman who caught a local pastor in the parking lot just before a wedding one Saturday night. She wanted milk for her child. Nothing was open except the chapel. At first the pastor ignored her the way Jesus did. He tried to walk past her. But his silence didn't deter her at all. So he tried excuses. "We're closed now, Ma'am. You'll have to come back Monday. Besides, I have this wedding to do." Jesus tried theology. "I was sent only to the lost sheep of the house of Israel." And with that line Jesus drew a very tight circle around himself. In essence, he was saying, I came to save Jews and that's all, lady, so go away and leave me alone.

But the woman wasn't put off with excuses or theology. She knelt before him and began to plead the way that mother began to plead with that pastor in the parking garage. "Please, don't you see that my daughter needs milk and she needs it now!" That's the way the Canaanite woman was talking to Jesus. You'd think that out of compassion his heart would have broken right there.

But Christ's humanity shows more here than anywhere else in the way he responded. Some think that we see his humanity on the cross when he says, "I thirst" and "My God, My God, why hast thou forsaken me." And we do, but I think we see Christ's humanity even more in his abrupt response to human need at this point in scripture.

It's as if God has no time for those who come to religion only when they're hurting and then turn their backs on God again once they get their basic needs met. However this woman has come, Jesus deals with her more harshly than he does anyone else in need in the New Testament. In essence, he calls her a dog, which is the derisive Jewish term for Gentile, which is what she was. "It's not right," says Jesus, "to take the bread meant for children and throw it to the dogs (of which you're one)." Here we see Jesus' own inner struggle over his own true mission. He wants to help the woman. That's his nature as God among us. But he also wants to honor his mission to the Jewish people. And as a good Jew, he is as cautious around Canaanites as modern Israelis would be around Saddam Hussein.

The reasons for racism are as varied as the faces of the world, and histories of pain inflicted one upon another are not easily or quickly forgotten. So part of the point of this story is that racism is hard to overcome even in the Son of God. And if it's hard for Jesus imagine how hard it is for us!

Most people would have folded at this harsh rebuke, especially from such a holy man. But the woman shows her true colors and actually teaches the Messiah a thing or two about his ministry. She expands his theology of mission beyond Israel to all the world. From this point on in Jesus' ministry, the mission is to be extended to wherever it encounters true faith that will not give up no matter what happens. This is faith that is not put off by the silence of God or the abruptness of God or God's representatives here on earth who seem to have their own agendas with places to go and couples to marry. Instead of being offended, she plows on. Why? Because she is willing to receive help no matter what Jesus' attitude toward foreigners may be. So she replies with a line that catches Jesus completely off guard and says, "Even dogs get crumbs from the master's table." Not only was she persistent, but in this line she demonstrated her quick wit. Like Churchill, Jesus was the master of retort, but that day he met his match in this lowly Canaanite woman and she beat him not really with her wit, but with her deep faith which Jesus recognized immediately.

So said Jesus in so many words, "Woman, you've got guts to talk to me like that!" But notice, instead of saying "Great is your wit, or great is your need," he said, "Great is your faith." It was her great faith that opened Jesus' heart: her deep, abiding and persistent faith in the incredible power of God that opened his mind to a new and exciting vista for his own ministry and for the future of Christianity. It was her great hope that opened Jesus' heart for, says Buttrick, "The expectancy that hopes great things of God is the passport to the kingdom (George Buttrick, *Interpreter's Bible,* vol. 7, Nashville, Abington Press, 1951, p. 442)." Finally, it was her love of God and her love for her child that opened the heart of the Messiah to do something great for her, to change his plans and later his mission.

So that night in the parking lot, that woman from the outside finally got through to that pastor. Her persistent faith, hope and love would not let him go as she pled for milk for her daughter. So they held up the wedding to find the formula, and you know, not a single person seemed to mind. As she headed out on foot to find and feed her baby, "She said with a smile, thank you, thank you, thank you so much. Thank you so much."

The faith of outsiders catches all of us off guard. How did the woman know what Jesus would do? She knew because she saw in him the power of God that could overcome her racism and his and a power that could do that could surely heal her daughter. And sure enough, it did.

The persistent faith of outsiders. If only we who claim to be on the inside had that kind of faith, imagine what God could do with us! Just imagine.

**Proper 16
Pentecost 14
Ordinary Time 21
Matthew 16:13-20**

Rocky

It is said that Winston Churchill never liked talking to subordinates. He always wanted to go to the top because he figured that was the only way he could get any action. So, as the story goes, when Churchill went to heaven, he met St. Peter at the gate and said, "Who are you?" When Peter said, "I'm St. Peter," Churchill said, "To hell with you, get God!"

How did poor Peter get this job in the first place? It all started with the story recounted in this text when Jesus renamed him "Rocky" and gave him the keys to the kingdom. Actually he called him Cephas which is an Aramaic nickname which means rock. Its Greek counterpart is Petros which also means rock. Thus on that day at Caesarea Philippi about 20 miles north of the Sea of Galilee, Simon Johnson, as he was known to his fishing buddies and his family, got a new name and his new name was Rocky.

Rocky was the big one, bigger than lifelike boxers by that name: Marciano or the character Sylvester Stallone played in the movie called *Rocky* and all its sequels. I can just hear him calling the other disciples with a tough Philadelphia street kid accent, "Hey you'se guys, let's go get some fish."

Rocky was aggressive, loud, bombastic, a ne'er-do-well who always wanted to be somebody, but he wasn't sure what. He'd do anything to make a name for himself. But he was stuck catching fish and living with his mother-in-law, and this Jesus, the street preacher from Nazareth, was his ticket out. So when the carpenter called to him from the shore one day when he was knee-deep in nets, he said, "Hey, why not?" and set out on the greatest adventure of his life. You can almost hear the theme song for the movie *Rocky* bursting forth in the background.

Rocky was the big one, bigger than life. In fact, Rocky was big in three ways that make you wonder why Jesus made *him* the rock on which he built the church and gave *him* the keys to the kingdom. Rocky was big in three ways.

First of all, he was a big bumbler, which should endear him to us immediately when we think of all the ways we have made a mess of our Christian lives; all the times we have tried to do the right thing in our lives and blown it and figured, "Well, that does it. Surely God is going to give up on me now." Surely I've had my last chance. About the time we think we're doing everything pretty well, we go and pull a boner. 'Course Peter never did it halfway. When he made a mistake, he did it so everyone could see and hear it loud and clear. Rocky was the kind who never looked at his bulletin so that when they got to the hymns he sang with great gusto when all the women and children were supposed to be singing, not aware at all until someone pointed it out after the service. That's the kind of thing Rocky would do. He rarely made little mistakes. His were always the kind everyone could see.

Peter wasn't a pretty Christian with everything in line. He was rough-hewn like a rock. Buechner is right: "A rock isn't the prettiest thing in creation or the fanciest or the smartest, and if it gets rolling in the wrong direction, watch out . . . (Frederick Buechner, *Peculiar Treasures*, New York, Harper and Row, Publishers, 1979, p. 134)." That's why being called a rock wasn't the greatest thing Jesus could do for Peter. A rock could mean a solid foundation, but it could also mean a stone of stumbling, the kind of "scandalon" that Paul talks about later. So it is for us in our Christian lives. Sometimes it seems like we're really holding the fort down for God and the kingdom in the ways we act and in the ways we treat each other. And at other times it seems like we're just in the way. A stumbling block. A real blockhead.

You ever feel like that? Like everything you do turns out wrong? You're trying your best to do what's right, but you just can't seem to get it right. That's the way Peter was, and I suppose it's at least small comfort that Peter blew it over and over again and was still named a saint and has survived the microscopic inspection of demythologization. Peter not only got in the way the way a rock sometimes does, he got stuck in his ways. Rocks have a tendency to do that. They have a tendency to solidify, to petrify, which heightens the difference between Peter and Paul, and Peter and Jesus.

Jesus was talking about something entirely new. Peter wanted to stay with the old like the hardliners in the former Soviet Union. Jesus was the utopian, Peter the conservative. Frank and Fritzie Manuel, in their book *Utopian Thought in the Western World,* suggest, "The utopian often emerges as a (person) with a deeper understanding of the drift of his society than the hardheaded problem-solvers with their noses to the grindstone of the present, blind to potentiality (George Keller, *Academic Strategy,* Baltimore and London, The Johns Hopkins University Press, 1983, p. 100)."

Remember Peter with Jesus at the mountain of transfiguration? Jesus is changed, transfigured, glorified. He is talking about where he is going, about new life. And all Peter wants to do is to freeze the moment. He wants to build a booth around it and keep it safe. "Peter, the rock, the brick-and-stone believer, the builder, the contractor . . ." wants to keep everything exactly as it is. And Jesus kept having to say, "Peter, you knucklehead. Get out of my way! Don't you see where I'm going with all of this?"

"There's not a lot you can do to change a rock or crack it or get under its skin, and, barring earthquakes, you can depend on it about as much as you can depend on anything. So Jesus called him the Rock, and it stuck with him the rest of his life. Peter, the Rock (Buechner, *op. cit.*)." And on this rock, on this knucklehead, said Jesus, I will build my church, which should give us all hope to see that Jesus would pick such a bumbler as Peter to be the foundation-stone for his church.

But Peter was not only a bumbler; he was also a big talker. It's like the vacation church school kid who came up to his pastor one day during the week and said, "You're the guy who's always talking in church." That's the way Peter was, always spouting off about this subject or that. Always mouthing off about how much he could do on his own and how he didn't need anybody else. "I can walk on the water all by myself, thank you very much," and then sank like a rock because that's what rocks do in the water, weighted down by their own self-centeredness. "I can wash my own feet, Jesus, so you can keep your towel to yourself." "I can do it myself!" says the four-year-old and the first grader and the first day on the jobber and the elderly invalid. "I don't need anybody else," say so many in our time, "least of all God!" "I can make it on my own," say dear friends of ours who are sicker than they think or whose marital life is a shambles, but they're afraid to burden anyone else with their problems, so they suffer quietly and alone.

Peter especially thought he could make it on his own. And time and time again he blew it the way you and I do. We're such big talkers when we join the church. All these promises. All these things we're going to do for God. Right!

"No Jesus," said Peter, "no way that I would deny you." 'Course the bigger they come, the harder they fall. What was it that gave him away in that early morning dark? Was it his Galilean dress? The slave girl picked it out in a flash, "Look, he's one of them!"

Was it his Galilean accent? That was enough to do it by itself. You could tell a Galilean a mile away. All he had to do was open his mouth. It'd be like plopping someone from New Jersey down in the middle of Cajun country. Galileans had a heavy accent, so ugly an accent that they weren't even allowed to pronounce the benediction in the synagogue. No one could stand it. And the slave girl picked it out just like that. "I know you. You're one of them." And Peter, the big talker, said, "No way, lady. Never met the man."

Then came the cock-crow or was it the trumpet or was it the haunting cry of his own conscience? Whatever it was, Peter couldn't take it any more. He wept like a baby. The big talker who thought he was somebody, was now a nobody and routed by a slave girl at that! Down to the mat one more time and Rocky finally throws in the towel.

Somehow Jesus knows he will. Somehow he knows we all will when the chips are down. Jesus is no easy optimist. He looks at all of us, big talkers that we are and says, "I know that some of you are going to peter out, just like Peter himself." After all, where do you think the Peter Principle came from in the first place? "I know when it comes to your faith," says Jesus, "that most of you will rise to your level of incompetence. You won't witness. You won't share. You'll find excuses not to give of yourself sacrificially. I know all this."

Somehow Jesus knows all this and yet he still forgives us on the way to the cross. Why? Do you suppose he sees in us what he saw in Peter? Some spark of goodness, some spark of penitence? Do you suppose that he sees in us despite all our bumbling and all our big talk that, like Peter, we are ready to risk something for God?

Certainly Peter was a risk-taker. It was a risk to leave his stable income and head out to God-knows-where with a wild-haired street preacher who had no place to lay his head and who seemed set on turning everything upside down. It was an enormous risk to proclaim Jesus the Messiah, the Son of the Living God, especially at Caesarea Philippi which was full of religious symbolism. Not only was this the place of former Syrian Baal worship, and supposedly the birthplace of the Greek god Pan, the god of nature, but here also stood a temple built by Herod the Great for the worship of Caesar.

In short, Rocky, I mean Peter, was risking the accusation of blasphemy and treason which would have meant certain death when he called Jesus the Anointed One. Somehow he knew that a new regime was coming in and he couldn't stay with the hardliners anymore. Now it was time to move on into a new order, the new kingdom which God was inaugurating with the coming of Jesus. And now he was beginning to see it all more clearly. He could see the effect Jesus was having on the hardliners and he could see that history was changing right before his eyes as it has been in our world in recent years.

How similar that period of history was too our own. In Jesus' day the hardliners suddenly realized that they were losing control. So they tried one last effort, one last coup and their coup was the cross. And for a few dark days it seemed that evil had won. Even the faithful like Peter began to falter, but then something happened that so shocked the world that it changed history forever. Evil was defeated, and the people rose up for their leader was alive and had come back among them and the hardliners scattered for somehow they knew that now there would be no turning back. That's what Peter knew the moment he saw the empty tomb and saw his risen Lord and heard his command to "Feed my sheep." He knew that from this day forward the world would never be the same.

Nothing would stop him now. Nothing, nothing at all. Not even his own bumbling or his own big mouth. Now he was ready to risk his life if need be, the way those Russian protestors did in August 1991 because in so doing he could help bring in the new order that God was inaugurating right before his eyes. Now was the time to stand up and be counted for a cause greater than himself. No more timidity. No more denial. No turning back. Just the recognition that his strength came only from Christ. And on that strength Peter started a new life. And on that life Jesus started a new church and a new era in world history.

So, in the end, you see, Rocky came through. But that's not the question, is it? The question is, will you?

Proper 17 — Matthew 16:21-28
Pentecost 15 — Matthew 16:21-26
Ordinary Time 22 — Matthew 16:21-27

Living Sacrifices

If we're really honest we have to admit that Peter speaks for all of us when he rebukes Jesus for saying that he would soon suffer. The main reason Peter does this is that following a God who suffers means we will probably have to suffer, too. Sure enough we were right; for immediately after Jesus puts Peter in his place, he says, "Those who want to be my followers must first deny themselves, take up their crosses and follow me."

What Peter probably figured out right from the beginning was that he would have to sacrifice. Paul carried the thought a step further in Romans 12 when he said that we are called to be "living sacrifices" which may be one of the main problems people have with Christianity today.

Sacrifice is not a word we use much these days, is it? When was the last time you used it or thought about it in terms of your own life? When was the last time you sacrificed anything for anybody? Come to think about it, there's only one sport as far as I know where the term is actually used. Do you know which sport that is? You can almost hear Harry Cary announcing it over the radio, "And there it goes, a long fly ball to left; easy out, but the man on third tags up and trots home. Sacrifice fly."

What a great idea — you're out, but you helped someone else score a run. Baseball is one of the few sports where you lose but the team still gains. Do you remember the way comedian George Carlin spells it out in his routine about the contrast between the hardness of football and the softness of baseball? He says:

> *In football you **Tackle!** In baseball, you "catch flies..."*
> *In football you **Punt!** In baseball you "bunt..."*
> *Football is played on a **Gridiron!** Baseball is played on a "field..."*
> *In football you **Score!** In baseball you "go home..."*
> *In football you **Kill!** In baseball you "sacrifice..."*

Baseball may be the only sport where you actually can hear this word. It's one of the few places anywhere that you hear it in a self-centered, take-care-of-yourself, don't-worry-about-anybody-else society. In contrast to football, sacrifice may sound like a sign of weakness but I hardly think of any of the Atlanta Braves or Minnesota Twins as weak.

Baseball's one thing; life is quite another. Who sacrifices anything any more in a time like ours? Who really denies themselves and takes up crosses anymore? Actually sacrifice can lead to bitterness, especially when you thought you were trusting God's plan for your life and suddenly you realize that you have to sacrifice all your greatest hopes and dreams as burnt offerings on the high altar of the providence of God.

James Stewart is right *(The Gates of New Life,* Charles Scribner's Sons, 1940, p. 32). There are probably very few people in any church or neighborhood in this world who can say that life for them has turned out exactly as they had hoped. One of the most common experiences in life is for us to set our hearts on this goal or that purpose and then life hands us something totally different.

Here is a young man who wanted to be a lawyer; but his father died, and he had to leave school and work to keep things going at home. Here is a young woman who wanted to be a great doctor but was never admitted to medical school. Here is a businessman who had hoped all his life to make his business a great success; but the competition was much tougher than he had ever expected, and he soon found himself declaring bankruptcy. Here is a couple whose marriage is on the rocks. When it started out it was so sweet and good but now . . . now it's just not the same. There is not a person in any congregation who has not sacrificed a hope or a dream as burnt offering on the high altar of the providence of God.

But there can be a great discovery which most of the biblical characters figured out, especially old Job; and that is the disciplining touch of pain and disappointment that can positively enrich our lives even when things seem to go wrong. For God is with us no matter what painful sacrifice we experience as we deny ourselves and follow him. According to Paul in Romans 5, it's something about "rejoicing in our suffering."

Picture the scene in 2 Chronicles 29:27 where king Hezekiah is about to sanctify the house of the Lord. All the offerings have been prepared, the altar, everything. And the scripture says, "Then Hezekiah commanded that the burnt offering be offered on the altar. And when the burnt offering began, the song of the Lord began also with the trumpets."

Here is what happens in the discipline of sacrifice when we deny ourselves and follow Christ. Our hopes and dreams go up as burnt offerings, but with the ears of faith we hear the song of the Lord with the trumpets and are made stronger in the process.

Look at those who start out cocky or arrogant like Peter; when they experience the loss of a loved one or close friend as Peter did, something happens to them and others notice something different in them that they have never seen before — a new poise and dignity, a deeper serenity. What happened to change them? When the offering of their pain was laid on the altar of God, the sound of the trumpets playing the Lord's song began in their lives, a sound so serene that it lifted their hearts through the sacrifice.

Of course this isn't always the way it happens, is it? For many the sacrifice of hopes and dreams only leads to bitterness. And you can tell the ones who have never heard the Song of the Lord beginning with trumpets. These are the ones who are cranky and hard to live with, the ones who say "poor me," "look what life has done to me!" So sacrifice can lead to deeper faith and peace and hope or it can lead to bitterness. It all depends on how you take it.

If the truth be known, we have to admit that we do make some sacrifices if only for ourselves or our own. We sacrifice for our children so they can go to school. We sacrifice here to buy something there. We sacrifice this snack now so we can eat that dessert later. And at fitness centers and on home treadmills or jogging tracks around the land, we present our bodies as living sacrifices week after week.

So we do sacrifice even if it is mostly for ourselves. But who sacrifices for others anymore? All kinds of people, when you think about it. Think of the scientists down through the years who have laid down their lives, victims of their own research for public health. Think how they deliberately contracted incurable diseases, exposed their bodies to radiation and to disease-carrying insects, and paid with their lives so that we might live.

Think of the troops sent to the Middle East, not knowing whether they would return. Someone asked one of the chaplains at Fort Hood in Texas, "How do your troops feel about it? Are they ready to fight?" The person wanted to know because that seemed to be the prevailing mood in the country. "No," the chaplain replied, "they're very anxious and unsure." They knew that they may have to sacrifice their lives for their country or was it for our way of life? Whatever the case, perhaps they, too, felt the sense of incompleteness the country feels over Vietnam, but like the commander over all the troops of Operation Desert Storm who also fought in Vietnam, they understood his comment when he said to a reporter: "Everyone loses in war. Everyone."

It is true, isn't it, that on occasion we find ourselves in a position to sacrifice, to lose our lives for others, whether in medicine or war, but who ever sacrifices for God any more? We don't think much about sacrificing for God, do we? The ancients did. Aztec history flows with the blood of human sacrifice. Interestingly, in an odd way their purpose was not too far from our predicament in the Middle East. Part of Aztec theology believed that if you had a little battle, just sacrifice a few of your own on the altar of the gods, it would actually deter a real war so that hundreds of thousands of others would live. Doesn't that sound a little like "lose a few hostages but in the process get Hussein and save millions of lives, not to mention our economy?" Sacrifice a few here to save millions there. It's good Aztec theology and on that theology they built their case for human sacrifices.

The ancient Hebrews sacrificed to appease God. But the watershed transition from human to animal sacrifice occurred in the story of the sacrifice of Isaac. You know the story — Abraham, tested by God, raised the knife to offer his own son but God stopped him and offered a lamb. The real point of this story is not the father's anguish; it was a great honor to offer your own son to God. No, the real point here is that among all the gods, this God no longer wanted human sacrifice. Not only that, he provided the sacrifice himself. And when you move to the New Testament, this same God startles us even more by providing the sacrifice again, this time not just a lamb, but his very own son.

In a dramatic reversal, God makes the ultimate living sacrifice himself for us. God presents his own body as a living sacrifice, holy and acceptable which is our spiritual service. That's what Jesus is saying to Peter and the other disciples. It's what Paul's little verse at the beginning of chapter 12 steeped with atonement theology is saying.

Because of God's sacrifice in Christ, we no longer offer humans or animals on bloody altars as our ancient American ancestors once did. Now in response to God's love in Christ, we offer ourselves. See the contrast Jesus and Paul set up between dead animals and our live bodies. But just as in the old Hebraic sacrifices, the offering cannot have a blemish (no lame or maimed goats or lambs), so with us (no spiritually half-dead lives). We can't come to God offering only part of ourselves, leaving the rest behind for the world to corrupt and manipulate. Just as baseball players who hit those sacrifice flies have to arrive at spring training in shape and ready to go, so we come before God saying, "Here I am, Lord, ready to go." And what does that mean? It means no longer being anxious or frustrated about the life God has given you. As some of your hopes and dreams have been sacrificed, somehow your life is still stronger yet, for you have begun to hear the Lord's song and the trumpets sounding.

Being a living sacrifice means to listen and care when others are hurting. It means to give until it hurts as a tither and then until it doesn't hurt anymore, since everything is God's anyway. It means to put God first above all else in our lives, which means above work or careers or cars or houses or sports (golf and tennis included as painful as that is) or television or video games (even Nintendo) or anything else in all creation. Being a living sacrifice, denying yourself and following Christ, means putting all those things on the altar of God if they stand in the way of God's purpose for your life and burning away your single-minded devotion to them. It means in Luther's words "letting goods, and kindred go, this mortal life also." It means doing something courageous in your life; stepping out and making a difference for others because in the end your whole life belongs to God.

It's like the woman Bruce Riggins met in London working in an amazing way with underprivileged people. When he asked her what had inspired her Christian faith and action, she shared her story of how seeing another Christian's faith converted her. She was a Jew fleeing the German Gestapo in France during World War II. She knew she was close to being caught and she wanted to give up. When she came to the home of a French Huguenot, a widow working with the underground came to tell her it was time to flee to a new place. This Jewish lady said, "It's no use, Ma'am, they'll find me anyway. They are so close behind." The Christian widow said, "Yes, they will find someone here, but it's time for you to leave. Go with these people to safety; I will take your identification and wait here."

Then the Jewish woman understood. The Gestapo would come and find this widow and think she was the fleeing Jew. As Bruce Riggins listened to this story, the now Christian woman of Jewish descent looked him in the eye and said, "I asked her why she was doing that and the widow responded, 'It's the least I can do; Christ has already done that and more for me.' " The widow was caught and imprisoned in the Jewish woman's place, allowing her time to escape. Within six months, the Christian widow was dead in the concentration camp.

The Jewish woman never forgot and became a follower of Christ through that one widow's living sacrifice. Who knows how many people will come to new life through the witness of your living sacrifice? What will it be for you? Mission field? Ministry? More committed service in your church or in your workplace? Only you and God can decide. Whatever it is, just do it. Present your body as a living sacrifice to God, holy and acceptable. Deny yourself and take up your cross and follow. How does that old hymn put it? Take my life and let it be, consecrated Lord to thee. And how about you? What are you doing these days to make your life a living sacrifice for Christ?

Proper 18
Pentecost 16
Ordinary Time 23
Matthew 18:15-20

Straight Talk, Due Process and Grace

It never ceases to amaze me how periodically someone joins the church thinking with great naivete that he or she has now left the imperfect, money-grubbing, power-hungry secular world and entered some holy, monastic community where everyone is good and kind and loving and no one ever gossips or spreads rumors or disagrees on any subject. When this happens, I usually watch to see how long it takes before this person's whole idyllic image of the church comes tumbling down like the proverbial deck of cards.

Usually, all it takes is serving on one committee or doing one job for the church. Whatever it is, sooner or later it happens. And then I watch what comes next: either total loss of enthusiasm and withdrawal, maybe a little sabbatical to regroup and re-evaluate or more church hopping, ever in search of that ever elusive, "perfect" church or, with some, it's complete abandonment and a return back into the more predictable secular world.

I never cease to be amazed at how perfect some people think the church is supposed to be. Presbyterians particularly shouldn't be so naive. After all, we believe in the depravity of humankind. It's good Calvinist doctrine. Pride and power will always creep in somewhere says Niebuhr, especially in the church. So, said Henry Ward Beecher, "I don't need John Calvin to tell me about total depravity, I have my own congregation to show me that!"

But some still join the church thinking that this isn't true. Pretty soon they begin to think that Jesus must have been misquoted. Surely, he must have meant to say "where two or more Christians are gathered in my name, there's bound to be an argument."

The interesting thing about Jesus is that though he was divinely incarnate, he was not divinely naive. He knew there were going to be disagreements and fights when well-meaning people got together in his name. He knew it wouldn't be easy. So in this passage he sets up a way for dealing with disputes.

Just as in a marriage, the issue was never whether there would be fights; the issue has always been whether folks were going to fight fair. A marriage, a friendship and a church are a lot alike in this area. The front of an anniversary card being sent these days to couples married 20 years or more spells out the four stages of marriage: The honeymoon, The shock of reality, The adjustment, and finally, The stage of quiet contentment. Inside it reads, "If you two don't hurry, you'll never get past the honeymoon stage!"

The fact is, sooner or later everyone gets past the honeymoon stage and if you can live through it all, if there is good communication and compatibility, you can grow to a richer and fuller depth of intimacy than ever experienced in the honeymoon because of honesty and understanding and real friendship, especially in the crisis moments, and there will be crisis moments. It's not a marriage without them. Unfortunately, not all marriages get this far and for them there should be nothing but lots of love and support especially in the church.

Just as in a marriage, so in a church there will be fights and disagreements. That's not the issue, says Jesus. The issue is, "Will you fight fair?" And what Jesus is doing in this passage very simply is laying down some ground rules, if you will, for "fighting fair." It's a kind of theological Robert's Rules of Order. Basically what Jesus is saying, is that we should never tolerate any situation in which there is a breach of personal relationships between us and another member of the Christian community. When something goes wrong what do we do about it? What Jesus is doing here is presenting a whole scheme of action for the mending of broken relationships within the Christian fellowship.

How does he spell it out? First of all, he recommends straight talk. That's one of the differences between the Midwest or the Southwest and say, the Southeast. In the Midwest or Southwest, people tell you straight out if there's a problem, in the Southeast, you have to go around the barn to find out. Straight talk, says Jesus, is prescription number one. You've got a problem with someone or something in the church? Deal with it directly. Don't embarrass that person in public — deal with it one-on-one if you can. Don't do it on the telephone; certainly not in a letter. Words on paper can be misinterpreted. Do it in person; and don't beat around the bush or sugarcoat it. Get right to it.

But that's so hard for some of us to do. So we don't or we talk behind others' backs, tear them down without them ever knowing about it or getting a chance to respond in person. If you've got a problem with someone and you don't have the gumption to go to that person yourself, then keep it to yourself. More harm has been done to others with "I shouldn't be telling you this, but did you know . . .?" than with any other line in the church. Leviticus 19, as a prelude to the famous "love thy neighbor as thyself," says "You shall not go up and down as a slanderer among your people . . ."

What Jesus is saying is this: "If your brother does wrong or your sister makes a mistake or you have a problem, speak to them for heaven's sake." Speak, speak, speak; don't keep your mouth shut. You will be held responsible for your silence and for the consequences of your unwillingness to speak.

Once a member of a seminary board shared a concern with an older member. "Share it with the board," said the old man abruptly. "Oh, I don't know," said the younger one, "I'm fairly new. I don't know if I should." The now retired president of a large management firm looked his younger counterpart in the eye and said, "There are times in my life when I could have spoken up and didn't; now I regret it. State your piece." So the timid, fledgling did and to his surprise, it resulted in a significant change in seminary policy on that subject and a change that should have occurred much earlier.

But it's so hard to do, you say. Of course it is. So we don't, or we do it around behind the scenes in destructive ways or we store up all our problems, which is called gunnysacking and dump them out on some poor soul or group when we really originally had only one item of contention. Bosses often do this to employees and spouses especially do it to each other. Straight talk without pretense or hidden agenda is so hard for some of us that we either gossip or gunnysack.

But for some of us, it's not hard at all. In fact, we rather enjoy taking our spouses, our children, our employees and friends and, yes, even fellow church members down a notch or two. The trouble is we seem to enjoy it too much. George Bernard Shaw was such a person. While he was still a music critic, he was dining with a friend one night in a restaurant that provided as entertainment an orchestra that was at best mediocre. The leader, recognizing Shaw, wrote him a note asking him what he would like the orchestra to play next. Shaw replied, "Dominoes."

Of course, Shaw met his match for speaking straight when he took on Churchill. Shaw once sent Churchill two tickets to the opening night of his play, *Saint Joan* with this note, "One for yourself and one for a friend — if you have one." Churchill replied expressing regret at being unable to attend, but asking for tickets for the second night, "that is, if there is one." And then, of course, there's the famous old rivalry between Lady Astor and Churchill where with some exasperation she said, "Winston, if I were married to you, I'd put poison in your coffee," to which Churchill replied, "And, if you were my wife, I'd drink it!"

Some people seem to have no trouble talking straight. In fact, the trouble is they seem to enjoy it too much. I don't think that this is what Jesus or Paul had in mind. Paul says when you have to speak the truth to a loved one, a friend or a fellow church member, speak the truth in love.

In a way that's what preaching and teaching are week after week in a local church. They are straight talk about scripture with nothing held back. It's what preachers and teachers are called on to do all the time. Sometimes it's uncomfortable for ministers to have to say a hard word to their congregations about the great gap between the way they're living and what God wants. The freedom of the pulpit and the teacher's podium involves an awesome responsibility which we should never abuse; but unfortunately some do. In attempting to talk straight, some preachers sound like stricken Elijahs as they scold their people. Usually their congregations let them know when they get too close to that. If they don't, you can be sure their spouses or at least close friends do.

Paul, carrying on the true intention of Jesus, says speak the truth in love, for in the end it is a good word, isn't it? Malcolm Muggeridge once put it this way: "Though this life at times seems like the theater of the absurd, there is a point where you realize that there is a reality, a meaning that as Blake's fine phrase suggests, life is the theater of fearful symmetry, there's something going on here which is real" and it's our job as preachers and teachers to help our congregations see the truth that our existence on this earth is not the whole story, for "in existing we fulfill the purpose of our creator which is a loving purpose, not a maligning purpose, a creative purpose, not a destructive purpose, an eternal purpose, not a temporal one." (This was said in a television interview with Bill Moyers on the Public Broadcasting Station.)

It's our job to speak that truth in a loving and genuine way even when the words are sometimes hard. So also in our relationships with one another.

If straight talk doesn't work in resolving the problem, then get others involved, says Jesus. It's due process. Take it to the elders. Try to settle it out of court with a few wise, patient, and loving friends. If that doesn't work, if the persons still refuse to listen, then be done with them. Show them the door. Treat them as gentiles or tax collectors. Treat them as you would a Saddam Hussein: no diplomatic relations.

There's only one problem with this approach. Jesus would never have said it. Practically all the commentators agree that this is the early church talking, working off the old rabbinical saying, "Love thy neighbor, hate thine enemy." But Jesus has transformed that saying to "Love thy neighbor as thyself and even love thine enemy."

So how do you deal with one with whom you have a problem? Talk straight first, speaking the truth in love. If that doesn't work, get others involved. When that fails, don't take the early church's advice; go with the intention of Jesus' full gospel message. In the end, remember grace. Grace is the bottom line when dealing with conflict because you never know how your actions and words toward another are going to affect the world.

In a little church in a small village, an altar boy serving the priest at Sunday Mass accidentally dropped the cruet of wine. The village priest struck the altar boy sharply on the cheek and in a gruff voice shouted "Leave the altar and don't come back." That boy became Tito, the Communist leader. In the cathedral of a large city in another place another altar boy serving the bishop at Sunday Mass also accidentally dropped the cruet of wine. With a warm twinkle in his eyes, the bishop gently whispered, "Someday you will be a priest." Do you know who that boy was? Archbishop Fulton Sheen.

How do you deal with others who have caused problems for you? Jesus has the answer. With straight talk, due process, but most of all, with grace. In so doing, you will fulfill more than the law and the prophets; you will fulfill the gospel of Jesus Christ.

Proper 19
Pentecost 17
Ordinary Time 24
Matthew 18:21-35

Who's Keeping Score?

What we have in our passage is the contrast between a theology of grace and a theology of keeping score. The first is the one Jesus espouses in this text. The second is the one Peter is pushing and, by the way, the one our world has bought into for centuries.

Anne Herbert once suggested that the whole thing started in Eden when Adam and Eve began keeping score. Certainly it was carried on in their children when Cain's anger over Abel's higher giving score finally led to murder. Anyway, God got so angry with Adam and Eve for worrying about their scores and which one had the bigger house or the newer car that he just kicked them out of Eden. It was, of course, the serpent who taught them how to keep score in the first place.

So, concludes Anne Herbert's parable (publisher unknown), "Really, it was life in Eden that didn't mean anything. Fun is great in its place, but without scoring there's no reason for it . . . We were lucky to get out. We're all very grateful to the snake."

So who's keeping score? Everybody is. God is horribly naive to think we aren't or don't want to. Who's keeping score? Ask any coach of any sport, you name it. Ask Ivan Lendl or John McEnroe. Do you expect any one of them to say, "Oh we had a wonderful time today. After all, it's not whether you win or lose; it's how you play the game that counts." Can you imagine Vince Lombardi saying such a thing?

Ask the head of any business. "Oh, we're just having fun here. It doesn't matter how much money we make." Ask CPAs and church treasurers. Ask politicians. I once sat in the hotel room with a gubernatorial candidate, watching the returns as he lost his first campaign. The room got very quiet. And a woman yelled out "Well, who wants to be governor anyway?" And the poor candidate said with a half smile "Well, I did. I did."

Who's keeping score? Everybody is. Surely, God is too. Surely, God isn't totally laissez-faire. Surely, God isn't some divine Zorba the Greek calling all of us to hedonistic frivolity. Surely, God is less epicurean and more stoic than that. Give us a good stern, Puritanical, Calvinistic God who cares when we are sinful, a God who cares how we act, who shows us that there are consequences to our actions; that the sins of the fathers and the mothers are passed on to the sons and the daughters, from generation to generation.

If God doesn't care, what difference does it make what we do? Surely God is keeping score in some way. Jesus seems to say that as he throws in this surprise at the end of the passage to call us up short, to catch all us Libertarians off guard who think we can sin with reckless acquisitiveness, and not care for the poor, just going through life getting by with murder (which is the way some have misread Paul). Jesus leaves us all hanging. Which is it, free grace — la de da? Or is there some bite to the gospel? Some accountability to the whole thing? We seem caught in the crossfire between the two churches across the street from one another in the same small town. One says, "There ain't no hell." The other says, "The hell there ain't!" Which is it? What's Jesus driving at here?

We know the story. The servant is summoned before the king. He owes him about $10 million. The king knows he'd lose more on the bankruptcy lawyer than he'd get out of the poor guy by taking him to court, so he tears up the debt and sends him away. The same servant goes out and roughs up the fellow who owes him $20. The king finds out, throws him in the slammer and throws away the key. Then comes the kicker. Jesus says, "So also my heavenly Father will do to every one of you, if you do not forgive your brother from your heart." Sure sounds to me like God's keeping score. Jesus seems to be saying here, God will not be mocked.

What's the deal here? Has Jesus gone hard on us? Or is this Matthew's own legalistic editorializing at the end? A downer that ruins the grace of the whole story? What is this: quid pro quo? Does all this mean if I don't forgive from the heart, God doesn't forgive me? No, it's not that simple. God cares what we do but God is not keeping score. Paul Rorem spells it out this way. "Few people think that God is an old man with a white beard on a throne; but some think he acts that way. As if God is up in heaven, looking down for unforgiving attitudes. 'Aha! There's another. Mark that one down, Gabriel, no forgiveness for John down there.' (Paul Rorem, *Augsburg Sermons 2,* Minneapolis, Augsburg Publishing House, 1983, p. 228)." That's not the way it works anymore than the way the universe works. Look at gravity. If you do something stupid like stepping off a cliff, God doesn't say "I'm going to punish that person with a fall." "On the human level, a selfish and self-centered life results in loneliness," not so much by some special act of divine retribution where God zaps you from above" as by the inner logic of the heart — the inner logic of the way we were made to be. The cause and effect are tied together by the very nature of the created order," especially in relationship to forgiveness (Rorem, *op, cit.,* p. 228-229).

You see, it's not a matter of keeping score, because there's no way to keep a ledger on grace. But Peter couldn't catch on. He still wanted to keep score. He'd learned in the school of Jesus that forgiveness must take the place of revenge — he understood that — but he was still asking about limits, and yet not as much as the Jews of his day. The rabbis basically said, "Three strikes and you're out." A person may be forgiven once, twice, even three times, but anything beyond that is foolishness. The town drunk will just keep coming back. You know the type — converted at every revival. And you can understand the rabbis' reasoning. After all, how many chances can you give a person? Peter, wanting to be generous, went beyond the rabbis and said, "Seven? How about seven?" And Jesus said, "No, seventy-times seven."

You can almost see Peter doing it in his head. "Let's see: seventy times seven is, carry the four, 490." But we miss the point if we do it in our heads, don't we? Jesus says, "Don't do it in your heads; do it in your hearts. Why? Because forgiveness is always beyond calculation." If God is keeping score on you, you'd have lost long ago. Greek scholars actually argue about whether he said seventy times seven or seventy-seven times. Either way it doesn't matter. Who's keeping score? Either way the extravagance is incredible. It's the extravagance of God.

God did our math in his heart when he sent his Son to die on a cross — and that's why the place to start is not with the threat in verse 35 but with the unbelievable unmerited forgiveness of a God who does not keep score on us, a God who gives us not only second, third and fourth chances, but a string of them to infinity. God is like a mother who will never ever give up on us; a mother who loves us when we don't feel very lovable any more, a mother who accepts us when we feel like we have no place to turn. It's a love that's hard to accept, says Paul Tillich, especially when you don't have much to start with.

Think of the little Down Syndrome child at school one day who forgot it was his birthday, mostly because he was poor and his parents hadn't planned anything special. When the announcement of his birthday came across the loudspeaker at school, he was surprised. And when he opened his presents — some school supplies, erasers, pens, and a little pocket flashlight — he said with tears in his eyes, "This is the best birthday I've ever had" and carefully saved the wrapping paper for weeks.

God's love is like that. It hits us out of the blue like a surprise birthday party when we least expect it. It comes to us like $10 million when we knew we had nothing coming. All we have to do is accept it graciously and send God a "thank you" note by showing God we know what it means.

And what it means, of course, is no more keeping score with friends, or family, or even our enemies. It means no $20 limit on our forgiveness credits. It means not hoarding any of our $10 million. It means never saying again: "I'm sorry but I can never forgive him for that." or "I can't put up with it any more." "The next time she's going to get it." or "Forgiveness is just too good for them."

When you really learn "who's keeping score?" theology, it loosens you up and you begin to share it with others. You're not so uptight about life, because you're not keeping a ledger on what others have done to you. Even those who are dead and gone. Think about that person in your life who has hurt you the most. Each of us has at least one. Now, let it go into God's hands.

Two things about our lives. They are irreversible and they are short. So we do what we can with what we have left, to make our peace with God, ourselves and those around us. We pray "forgive us our debts as we also forgive our debtors their debts to us." We pray that and then we try to live it.

I'm sorry but I can't spell it out for you, says Walter Burghardt. "It's not for me to say to a survivor of Auschwitz: Forgive the Nazi who gassed your parents. It's not for me to tell a rape victim, forgive and forget. It's not for me to tell you to sit down and cancel all your debts. A sermon, like a parable, has different lessons for different listeners, different strokes for different folks (Walter Burghardt, *Sir, We Would Like To See Jesus,* New York, Paulist Press, 1982, p. 113)." You have to decide for yourself.

For Toyohiko Kagawa it was the slums of Tokyo. For Dom Helder Camera, it's the slums of Brazil. For Mother Theresa it was the slums of Calcutta. For Jesus Christ it was all humanity mired down in the slum of its own sin on Calvary.

As they taunted him and crucified him, I'm sure the disciples and others wondered why Jesus didn't retaliate. Whatever happened to good old divine retribution? Instead he hung there and took it. Why? Because long ago he figured out that God had stopped keeping score.

If God has stopped keeping score on us, why are we still keeping score on those around us? Father, forgive us, for we know not what we do.

Proper 20
Pentecost 18
Ordinary Time 25
Matthew 20:1-16

The Unfairness of God

Have you ever noticed how sometimes life just isn't fair? It's one of the hard realities we learn early on. No one has to wait for adolescence or old age to find it out. You can learn it in nursery school. Sometimes life just isn't fair.

Little brothers and sisters seem to get such special privileges. The things my little brother and sister got away with! There were times when I really felt like the prodigal son story was some kind of Jungian archetype for familial systems down through the centuries. Well, I didn't exactly put it that way when I was 15, but that's how I felt. It's the way older employees feel when young hot shots come into the workplace and the older ones get shoved out into unemployment lines. It's the way veteran athletes feel when rookies get drafted with multi-million dollar contracts while the veterans have been slugging it out at smaller salaries all these years. Some coaches even treat these rookies differently from the rest, giving them special privileges the way we sometimes do with our children or our employees or our students. Of course there was one coach who never did that. Once in commenting on Vince Lombardi's fairness, one of the Green Bay Packers noted that Lombardi treated every player the same. "He treats us *all* like dogs," said the player. Some coaches are fair, but many are not in their treatment of players, just as parents are not with children, employers with employees and teachers with students.

Sometimes that's just the way life is, which is in part the point of the parable of the laborers in the vineyard. Chances are most clergy and laity of congregations around America have never been migrant workers. If you have, perhaps you can hear this story at more of a gut level. But if you haven't, it doesn't take much imagination to figure how mad you'd be. Suppose you had signed on to pick fruit for eight hours at the rate of five dollars an hour, or $40 for the day — a fair day's wage for a fair day's toil. You work right through the heat of the day without letting up except for lunch. While making your way to the paymaster at five o'clock, you stand in line behind someone who showed up for work at four o'clock and who had only worked one hour.

You watch closely and see that she is paid $40 for her hour's work which sets your heart beating in anticipation. Naturally, you figure since you worked eight hours, you're going to get eight times as much. But when you get to the head of the line, open your pay envelope and find only $40, tell me how you are going to feel. Maybe not in the south, but in big union towns like Pittsburgh or Detroit, a deal like that wouldn't last five minutes. The word would be out on that employer, just like that! I don't know about you, but I'd be pretty upset.

But sometimes that's the way things happen, isn't it? Sometimes life just isn't fair. So we try to deal with the unfairness, like the little truck driver, just a little guy, who had parked his semi at the highway cafe and had gone in for lunch. While he was sitting there perched on a stool, three burly motorcyclists came in and began picking on him, grabbed his food away and laughed in his face. The truck driver said nothing, got up, paid for his food and walked out. One of the cyclists laughed to the waitress, "Boy, he sure wasn't much of a man, was he?" The waitress replied, "No, I guess not. He's not much of a truck driver, either," she said pointing out the window. "He just ran over three motorcycles."

You see, some handle the fairness of life by dealing with it directly, or at least indirectly, anyway. Others try to deal with it by just thinking positively. You know the type. No matter what happens to them, they always see the sunny side of things. Surely something good can come out of this. Like the boy who was overheard talking to himself as he strutted across the backyard, bat on his shoulder, baseball in his hand. Just before pitching the ball in the air he said, "I'm the greatest hitter in the world," swung and missed and said "Strike one!" Undaunted, he picked up the ball and tossed it up again and said, "I'm the greatest baseball hitter ever," swung and missed a second time and said "Strike two!" He paused a moment to look at the bat and ball carefully and with all the determination and positive mental attitude he could muster, he tossed it up again and said, "I'm the greatest hitter who ever lived," swung the bat hard, but missed it the third time. Immediately he cried out, "Wow! Strike three! What a pitcher! I'm the greatest pitcher in the world!"

That's what I call bouncing back quickly! Some deal with the unfairness of life by just thinking positively. Okay if I'm not supposed to do that, maybe I should be doing this or if I'm going to fail that way, maybe I should try it this way.

For some that works pretty well, at least for a time. Then life deals a blow that really lays us low, so low that it even brings the world's most positive thinkers down, even a Jean Valjean in Victor Hugo's *Les Miserables*. It usually comes when bad things happen to good people and they do and they will. The good do die young while the wicked sometimes live long and seemingly happy lives; the good do get cancer and suffer while the bad are often physically and emotionally healthy. The honest and upright do lose their jobs or their businesses, while the cheats and the liars seem to keep theirs. Sometimes life is so unfair that not even positive thinking can overcome it. Imagine trying to tell Job to think more positively about his situation. Try telling someone who's living on the street or someone whose loved one has just committed suicide because she can't take the cancer or the depression any more.

Sometimes life is so unfair we can't begin to understand it. And that's when we begin to question not just the fairness of life, but the fairness of God, which is what the laborers in the vineyard, Job, and the hearers of both stories, no doubt did. In fact, there are plenty of biblical figures who would be happy to join this parade. Here is Jeremiah: "O Lord, thou hast deceived me . . . Cursed be the day on which I was born!" Here is Habakkuk: "O Lord how long wilst I cry for help and thou wilst not hear? Or cry to thee 'Violence!' and thou wilst not save?" Here is Joseph in the Old Testament dumped in the pit and sold into slavery by his brothers and Mary in the New Testament eyeball to eyeball with Gabriel or was it the Holy Spirit demanding to know what kind of mess God had gotten her into. The Bible is full of folks who would love to tell us about the unfairness of God.

Add to this list the litany of all those who don't buy the deathbed confessions of serial killers or Nazi war criminals or slave owners in the old South. What kind of God is this, anyway? It's just not fair! Isn't this what we would call the offense of grace? Don't some of us now want to change the hymn to "Amazing grace how sorry the sound that saved a wretch like him." Whether it's Job or Job's friends or the laborers who had worked all day or Jeremiah or Mary or you or me, sooner or later we have to admit that there at least are some times in our lives when we wonder about the fairness of God.

But — and here is a crucial point of today's passage so don't miss it — *saying life isn't fair is not the same as saying God isn't fair* for two specific reasons. First, God doesn't owe us anything and second, God's justice doesn't work the way ours does.

Saying life isn't fair is not the same as saying God isn't fair because first of all God doesn't owe us anything. On the contrary, we owe God everything: our time, our talent, our money, even our very lives. The lives we live are lives that God has given to us; even the breath, each breath that we take in at this very moment, the clothes on our backs, the food on our table, our health in its varying degrees, since some of us do have ailing parts but at least we're here; the gifts of mind and body to do the jobs we've been called to do — all of that is the sheer gift of God. In addition to all this is the amazing grace given to us through Jesus Christ that is beyond all imagination. In the parable of the unforgiving servant (Matthew 18:23-35) the king forgave his servant's debt for 10,000 talents. In today's rate of exchange that would be about $10 million. That's a good way to think about grace. For our sin and for the trouble we have caused God, ourselves and others, at the check-out counter, the checker rings it all up and do you know what your bill is? It's the same as mine: $10 million. That's what we owe. And just as we are about to faint, God walks through and rips up the ticket, not only for those of us who have been faithfully working around the store all these years, but for the ne'er do well who walks in right off the street.

Our bill with God is so big we could never say "Hey God, you owe me. I deserve more of your grace, more of your love than the one next to me in the pew." The fact is, we don't deserve any of it because God doesn't owe us a thing. And when God doesn't owe us anything, we shouldn't begrudge God's acceptance of those who seem less deserving of God's love than those of us who have been slugging it out in the church all these years.

We shouldn't think of God's love lavished on no-goods and tramps and big time sinners as unfair because God's justice doesn't work the way the world's justice works. It's not so much that it contradicts the world's way of doing things as some separatist religious cults would have us believe. The justice of the world is good. We need it to order society. Both Karl Rahner, a Roman Catholic and David H. C. Read, a Presbyterian, believe that justice and love are within the purview of God. Both theologians highlight the importance of contracts in our world, of being fair, and of being paid what was agreed upon. When the laborers cried out, the master answered the outcry with a straightforward appeal to legality and justice. "Look, you got paid what we agreed on, didn't you?" No matter how unfair the world sometimes seems, God is fair the way the world at its best can be which is "each according to his due."

Here, the justice of the world and the justice of God correspond. God's love does not replace the justice of the world as some separatist groups would like to think. That's why this Thomistic and Calvinist approach is so realistic since it does not set God's justice over against the justice of the world. With the Thomist, Rahner, the social justice of "each according to his due" is not denied, but extended. Love and justice both come from the same source, but love takes justice further. So good laws and good contracts are good for the community, but God's love carries good laws even further. Social justice is given an even deeper meaning by God's incalculable mercy: for less than a day's work, more than a day's wage, is given, which does not seem fair by the world's standards but, in God's eyes, it is ultimately fair. So God is not only fair since we were paid what we agreed from the start, "each according to his due," but God is more than fair, "each more than she is due." This is the love of God transforming the justice of the world with what Reinhold Niebuhr called the transvaluation of values.

How does that transvaluation occur in our lives? It makes us less jealous of latecomers and upstarts in the faith. It makes us less jealous of third world countries which represent now the church of the future and the future of the church. It makes us less jealous of illegal aliens and unwanted immigrants and little sisters who get special treatment. The point of this parable, believes Helmut Thielicke, is that no one will ever be able to see the goodness or the fairness of God with a jealous eye.

Worldly justice is not wrong. It just doesn't go far enough. God's benevolent justice not only does not contradict good contract justice; it goes beyond it and transforms it and in so doing becomes a model for us to be more just and more loving in our relationships with others like the old Bishop in *Les Miserables* who forgives Jean Valjean for stealing the silver and, in fact, says that he gave it to him in the first place and asks him why he left the two candlesticks behind to the shock and surprise of everyone, including Valjean himself.

God's grace is God's grace. It is the same for everybody. Since we don't earn it, it comes to us in different ways. To some it doesn't mean as much since we've been trying to live the right way all along. To others who haven't done a lot around a church or for others who have perhaps wasted nearly their whole lives and come to church late, God's grace means a lot more. But the gift of grace is all the same.

That may seem unfair to you, but it's not because God is more than fair, for in Jesus Christ, God took all the unfairness of our lives and our troubled world on himself and suffered the unfairness of death on a cross that we might have life. In church or hospital or home, in scripture, sermon and song, in Word and font and table, we meet this God who is not only fair but immeasurably kind.

In Jesus Christ we find that what seems to be the unfairness of God in saving those who don't seem to deserve it is in reality the grace of God for you and for me. So worry not about those who don't seem to deserve it. Remember that, except for God's grace in Christ, neither do we.

Remember that the kingdom of heaven is a gift. In a way we're all latecomers, aren't we? And in Christ it's never too late to come home to God.

Proper 21
Pentecost 19
Ordinary Time 26
Matthew 21:28-32

Church People Beware!

I don't know about you, but I don't think much of the choices Jesus offers in this passage. Think about it with me for a moment. Two sons. The father tells each one to go and do a little work in the vineyard. It's not much to ask, like mowing the lawn every once in a while. Parents don't ask their children to do that many chores around the house. Besides, it's the least they can do to earn their keep. So, says Jesus, this particular father asks his two boys to help out a little around the vineyard. But get this: one of them says "No," and then does it; the other one says "Yes, Dad, I'll be glad to," and then doesn't.

Kids . . . What are you going to do with them? Once you think you have them figured out, they either surprise you or they let you down. And part of the problem is that they're so hard to talk to. They seem to speak a different language which may be something of a cross between "rap" and a low mumble or they don't talk at all.

A father once tried to talk to his son about how college was going:

The father said, "How are things going?"
The son said, "Good."

The father said, "And the dormitory?"
He said, "Good."
The father said, "How are your studies going?"
He said, "Good."
The father said, "Have you decided on a major yet?"
He said, "Yes."
"Well, what is it?" asked the father.
The son said, "Communication."

So it goes as parents and children try to talk to each other. So it was for the two sons in Jesus' story. Personally, I don't think much of either son. Neither one did what he said he was going to do. But this isn't an Ann Landers or Erma Bombeck passage about the trials and tribulations of rearing children. It's really about the Pharisees and the Pharisee types who talk the talk but don't walk the walk.

Here goes Jesus again. You ever notice how Jesus seemed to enjoy picking on the Pharisees which wasn't really fair since they were the good people in their day. They were the ones with power and knowledge, the ones who were "upright, righteous, and right with God." They knew the law and actually kept it. It's not that they were completely sinless. Even they knew that everyone is tainted with Eden's damage. But they kept the laws of God as closely as was humanly possible. Not only that, they actually came to church every week. They read their Bible and even went to Bible studies. And, of course, they tithed and actually kept their pledges paid up, which made them real popular around the synagogue, especially with the rabbis.

So what was the problem? Why do you suppose Jesus picked on them? Maybe it was because they deserved it. In reality they were a pretty self-righteous bunch, holding everyone to the grindstone of every little jot and tittle of the law. Not only that, when you scratched the surface of their piety, you found that there wasn't much real commitment underneath. They were much more concerned with their own salvation and determining who was saved and who wasn't than they were with helping those who were really lost come into the presence of God. When was the last time you were concerned with that: helping someone who seemed to be lost to come into the presence of God?

The Pharisees weren't much interested in that. They were much more interested in themselves and their own ritual purity. They were big on promises about doing something for those in need, but not much on follow-through; big on saying, but not much on doing. It's like the black preacher who gave the sermon on the Good Samaritan and told about the priest who, traveling the same route as the man who had been beaten, had "passed by on the other side" and then the black preacher, "with moving eloquence, described how competent and comfortable the priest was in the Jerusalem temple. He could handle it all with practiced ease: the altar and the sacrifices, the vestments and the incense, the wood and the ashes — everything that had to do with the temple. No trouble there, no sweat. What he could not handle was the event on the Jericho road (Walter Burghardt, *Grace on Crutches,* New York, Paulist Press, 1986, p. 132)."

Here is a problem that catches most of us, especially preachers. We're great when we're hanging around the church on Sundays: prayers, hymns, sermons, Sunday school lessons, all the different jobs we do; but where we have trouble is in handling the events on the Jericho road. Where we have trouble is making something of our Christian lives where we live and work and play. Where we have trouble is in our relationships with our spouses and former spouses and our parents and our children and friends and fellow workers and even those in need whom we both fear and despise. We take vows as church leaders and members and promise all kinds of wonderful things and then go out and kick people in the teeth in the ways we treat them. That's happening in every congregation.

Don't you find a little bit of contradiction in that? God does. Jesus does. And he sees right through us, right through our little facades; and with this parable he says, "Church people beware!" James picked up the same theme later and played it out as far as it would go. You know the passages, "Faith without works is dead," and all that. But try as he wants, James could never go as far or state it as poignantly as Jesus did.

In fact, the more I read this passage the more nervous I get. I said to someone last week, "The first question I want to ask when I get to wherever I'm going after I die is, 'Why do the good ones suffer so much here on earth?' " We all have questions we want to ask. That's the one I want to ask. But then someone observed, "That's presuming you go to the right place." And I said, "Yeh, well, that's right . . . That's right!"

Imagine Jesus walking into your church on a Sunday morning (any Sunday will do), interrupting the service, standing right down front and saying, "The IRS types who have been overtaxing you and the harlots in the red light district who have cleaned up their acts and sincerely changed their ways but don't come to church every week have a better shot at heaven than you do." Well, Jesus never was very big on Dale Carnegie anyway. No wonder they were measuring him for a cross soon after he came to town.

Imagine him going on. Still standing down front since no one had moved and the ushers at the back didn't know what to do, kept staring up front for a signal from the preacher who by now looked a little pale; imagine Jesus going on with something like this: "Mahatma Gandhi had a better shot at heaven than most Americans who go to church every week because he really lived what I was trying to teach. And those who pour bowls of stew have a better shot at heaven than you who are so concerned to get the liturgy exactly right or are bickering over which hymns we're going to sing as if that makes any difference to God at all!"

Typical church people ought to be pretty nervous about this passage. I am. Preachers and teachers especially ought to be nervous. Neither teacher training nor a seminary degree is an automatic ticket to heaven. No one should arrogantly assume salvation. No one. What Jesus is saying is that those who don't profess faith but live it as if they have, have a better shot at salvation than those who profess but don't act.

Athenagoras, a Christian philosopher in Athens, once said it this way: "Among us are uneducated folks, artisans, and old women who are utterly unable to describe the value of our doctrines in word, but who attest them by their deeds (Bruce L. Shelly, *Church History in Plain Language,* Dallas, Word Publishing, 1982, p. 88)."

If we were to stop here with all this talk about the difference between saying and doing, and we were in a typical homiletics class, the critique would be that what we have said so far could not be classified as a sermon but a good pep talk that could be used anywhere. Now I realize it's not exactly the kind of rah-rah cheerleading message that you would hear at the local Rotary Club or Girl Scout meeting. Jesus was never really a saccharine motivational speaker. That just wasn't his style. But if we took his message the way some in our day try to do and failed to see it in its proper Christological context, all we would get would be this: "Follow through on your promises," which is not a bad message in itself, especially for church folk whether in pulpit or pew; it's pretty straightforward. The only trouble is it's not really a sermon.

The main problem here is that the contrast in this passage is not just between saying and doing. The contrast is between accepting or rejecting Christ. The Pharisees never did. And sadly, many church people never do either. Oh they come, some even regularly. But they never really accept what it means to be "in Christ." And what does it mean? It means getting to know the mind of Christ, his harsh judgment and his great mercy. It means experiencing the grace of Christ by truly repenting and being sorry for our sins, especially as we come to the Lord's table. Finally, it means living the life of Christ every day by thinking of others, especially those in need, before we think of ourselves.

What about you? Which have you done in your life? Accepted Christ or rejected him not just in your words but in the way you live your life and the way you treat those around you? Have you really accepted the Christ who challenges you and comforts you all at the same time?

Every once in a while you meet someone who was at a table like this one. Cleo McClure did, an elderly woman in our church who died a while back. She was quiet, unassuming, humble, and generous to a fault. She hadn't been able to come to church for years but she believed it and she lived it like the saints. Not long ago I saw her for the last time. We shared communion around a table like the one in every church. She was moved to tears as we said the 23rd Psalm, words that came out from deep inside her as she recited them with me. Here was one who not only knew the psalm, but knew the shepherd. Why was she in tears? Was it because she knew she was about to meet her maker? I don't know. But I do know this. She came to the table of the Lord for her last time in penitence and hope. She came to the table accepting the sustenance of Christ, which is what we should do every time we partake of the sacrament.

Don't come to the Lord's table unless you mean it, for the Lord's table is set with an invitation and a warning. The invitation is only to those who are truly sorry for their sins. The warning is to those who casually assume that they have the salvation of God and they think they know who doesn't. So the warning is not so much "Sinners beware" as it is "Church people beware! Don't come to the table of the Lord unless you mean it."

Lectionary Preaching After Pentecost

Virtually all pastors who make use of the sermons in this book will find their worship life and planning shaped by one of two lectionary series. Most mainline Protestant denominations, along with clergy of the Roman Catholic Church, have now approved — either for provisional or official use — the three-year Common (Consensus) Lectionary. This family of denominations includes United Methodist, Presbyterian, United Church of Christ and Disciples of Christ.

Lutherans and Roman Catholics, while testing the Common Lectionary on a limited basis at present, follow their own three-year cycle of texts. While there are divergences between the Common and Lutheran/Roman Catholic systems, the gospel texts show striking parallels, with few text selections evidencing significant differences. Nearly all the gospel texts included in this book will, therefore, be applicable to worship and preaching planning for clergy following either lectionary.

A significant divergence does occur, however, in the method by which specific gospel texts are assigned to specific calendar days. The Common and Roman Catholic Lectionaries accomplish this by counting backwards from Christ the King (Last Sunday after Pentecost), discarding "extra" texts from the front of the list: Lutherans follow the opposite pattern, counting forward from The Holy Trinity, discarding "extra" texts at the end of the list.

The following index will aid the user of this book in matching the correct text to the correct Sunday during the Pentecost portion of the church year.

(Fixed dates do not pertain to Lutheran Lectionary)

Fixed Date Lectionaries *Common and Roman Catholic*	**Lutheran Lectionary** *Lutheran*
The Day of Pentecost	The Day of Pentecost
The Holy Trinity	The Holy Trinity
May 29-June 4 — Proper 4, Ordinary Time 9	Pentecost 2
June 5-11 — Proper 5, Ordinary Time 10	Pentecost 3
June 12-18 — Proper 6, Ordinary Time 11	Pentecost 4
June 19-25 — Proper 7, Ordinary Time 12	Pentecost 5
June 26-July 2 — Proper 8, Ordinary Time 13	Pentecost 6

July 3-9 — Proper 9, Ordinary Time 14	Pentecost 7
July 10-16 — Proper 10, Ordinary Time 15	Pentecost 8
July 17-23 — Proper 11, Ordinary Time 16	Pentecost 9
July 24-30 — Proper 12, Ordinary Time 17	Pentecost 10
July 31-Aug. 6 — Proper 13, Ordinary Time 18	Pentecost 11
Aug. 7-13 — Proper 14, Ordinary Time 19	Pentecost 12
Aug. 14-20 — Proper 15, Ordinary Time 20	Pentecost 13
Aug. 21-27 — Proper 16, Ordinary Time 21	Pentecost 14
Aug. 28-Sept. 3 — Proper 17, Ordinary Time 22	Pentecost 15
Sept. 4-10 — Proper 18, Ordinary Time 23	Pentecost 16
Sept. 11-17 — Proper 19, Ordinary Time 24	Pentecost 17
Sept. 18-24 — Proper 20, Ordinary Time 25	Pentecost 18
Sept. 25-Oct. 1 — Proper 21, Ordinary Time 26	Pentecost 19
Oct. 2-8 — Proper 22, Ordinary Time 27	Pentecost 20
Oct. 9-15 — Proper 23, Ordinary Time 28	Pentecost 21
Oct. 16-22 — Proper 24, Ordinary Time 29	Pentecost 22
Oct. 23-29 — Proper 25, Ordinary Time 30	Pentecost 23
Oct. 30-Nov. 5 — Proper 26, Ordinary Time 31	Pentecost 24
Nov. 6-12 — Proper 27, Ordinary Time 32	Pentecost 25
Nov. 13-19 — Proper 28, Ordinary Time 33	Pentecost 26 Pentecost 27
Nov. 20-26 — Christ the King	Christ the King

Reformation Day (or last Sunday in October) is October 31 (Common, Lutheran)

All Saints' Day (or first Sunday in November) is November 1 (Common, Lutheran, Roman Catholic)

www.ingramcontent.com/pod-product-compliance
Lightning Source LLC
Chambersburg PA
CBHW060852050426
42453CB00008B/946